EXCAVATE!
DINOSAURS

written by
Jonathan Tennant

illustrated by
Vladimir Nikolov

paper engineering by
Charlie Simpson

Storey Publishing

United States edition published in 2014 by

Storey Publishing

210 MASS MoCA Way

North Adams, MA 01247

www.storey.com

The mission of Storey Publishing is to serve our customers by publishing practical information that encourages personal independence in harmony with the environment.

The information in this book is true and complete to the best of our knowledge. All recommendations are made without guarantee on the part of the author or Storey Publishing. The author and publisher disclaim any liability in connection with the use of this information.

Storey books are available for special premium and promotional uses and for customized editions. For further information, please call 1-800-793-9396.

ISBN: 978–1–61212–520–6

Copyright © 2014 Ivy Press Ltd

This book was conceived, designed & produced by

Ivy Press

CREATIVE DIRECTOR	Peter Bridgewater
COMMISSIONING EDITOR	Georgia Amson-Bradshaw
MANAGING EDITOR	Hazel Songhurst
PROJECT EDITOR	Judith Chamberlain-Webber
ART DIRECTOR	Kim Hankinson
DESIGNER	Joanna Clinch
ILLUSTRATORS	Vladimir Nikolov and Charlie Simpson
PAPER ENGINEER	Charlie Simpson

Font credit   WC Rhesus

Printed in China

Color origination by Ivy Press Reprographics

10 9 8 7 6 5 4 3 2 1

Contents

Cretaceous Period

Jurassic Period

Triassic Period

IT'S YOUR TURN TO BE A PALEONTOLOGIST!

Paleontologists are scientists who study fossils, the preserved hard parts of animals or plants that lived on Earth many millions of years ago. Dinosaur remains are among the most famous discoveries, and everything that paleontologists know about these amazing creatures comes from their fossilized bones.

But how do paleontologists figure out which bones belonged
to which dinosaur? Reconstructing a complete dinosaur
is like doing a 3D puzzle—without a picture. And many
dinosaurs are only known from a few fossils, which makes
rebuilding them quite a challenge.

Now it's your turn! In the Field Guide section of
this book, you'll find details on 12 dinosaurs. As a
paleontologist, your job is to study the scientific
information carefully and use it to identify and collect
the pop-out fossil pieces in the Dig Sites section. Then
you can reconstruct your very own 3D dinosaur models!

WHAT WERE DINOSAURS?

Dinosaurs were the primary land animals approximately 235 to 66 million years ago, a time spanning most of the Mesozoic era. At the end of the Mesozoic era, all dinosaurs, except for the ancestors of modern birds, became extinct.

HOW LONG AGO?

The Mesozoic era can be divided into three periods: the Triassic, the Jurassic and the Cretaceous. Before the Mesozoic was the Paleozoic era, and after it, the Cenozoic. This timeline shows each era, the periods within the eras, and some of the life forms that evolved.

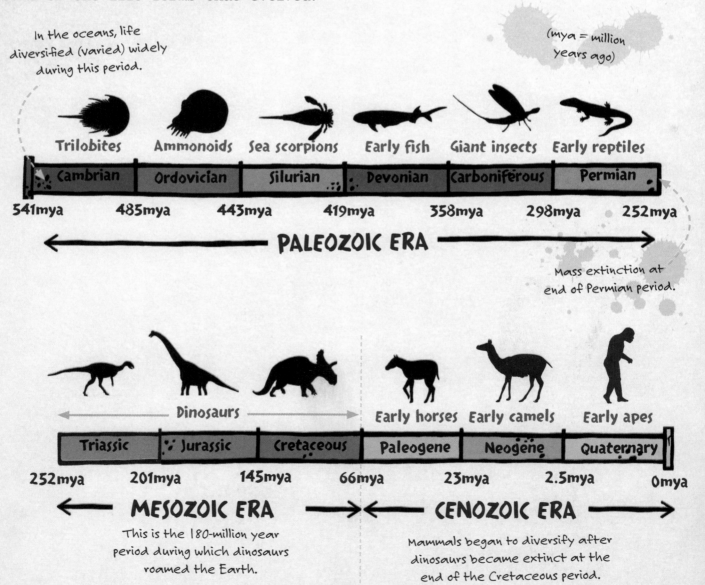

In the oceans, life diversified (varied) widely during this period.

(mya = million years ago)

Trilobites — Ammonoids — Sea scorpions — Early fish — Giant insects — Early reptiles

| Cambrian | Ordovician | Silurian | Devonian | Carboniferous | Permian |

541mya — 485mya — 443mya — 419mya — 358mya — 298mya — 252mya

← PALEOZOIC ERA →

Mass extinction at end of Permian period.

Dinosaurs — Early horses — Early camels — Early apes

| Triassic | Jurassic | Cretaceous | Paleogene | Neogene | Quaternary |

252mya — 201mya — 145mya — 66mya — 23mya — 2.5mya — 0mya

← MESOZOIC ERA → ← CENOZOIC ERA →

This is the 180-million year period during which dinosaurs roamed the Earth.

Mammals began to diversify after dinosaurs became extinct at the end of the Cretaceous period.

THE FIRST DINOSAURS

The earliest dinosaurs were small, two-legged animals. Over time, they developed into a wide variety of forms and sizes, from the giant sauropods that could be more than 164 ft (50m) long to the tiny *Fruitadens* that were just 26 in (65cm) long—about the size of a small dog!

Some dinosaurs were bizarre, with bony plates or spikes along their neck and back.

Fruitadens was covered in long bristles. Its tapering tail was longer than its body.

Ankylosaurus had armored plates and a heavy "club" on the end of its tail.

Anchiornis had feathers, allowing it to glide.

Giraffatitan, one of the sauropods, had an enormously long neck for grazing on tall plants.

THE LAST DINOSAURS...

Dinosaurs were on Earth for around 180 million years! After they became extinct approximately 66 million years ago, mammals became the dominant lifeform, along with the descendants of dinosaurs—birds.

WHAT ARE FOSSILS?

We learn about animals that lived millions of years ago by studying fossils, which are the remains and traces of dead animals and plants buried and preserved within rocks, sometimes for hundreds of millions of years.

HOW WERE FOSSILS MADE?

Conditions had to be just right for a dead animal to be fossilized. It had to be buried quickly, far away from things that would normally make it decay, or creatures that would eat it. These circumstances kept the body in good condition.

Once buried, the animal's bones and other hard body parts were gradually replaced by minerals, creating fossils.

Fossils can be anything from bacteria and tiny insects ...

... to the largest dinosaurs.

WHERE TO FIND FOSSILS

Fossils are usually found in sedimentary rock. This type of rock is created when water dumps tiny fragments of rock, mud and other materials (sediment) to form layers that are eventually squeezed together into rock.

If you dug down through layers of sedimentary rock, you would be digging through time.

DIGGING DOWN

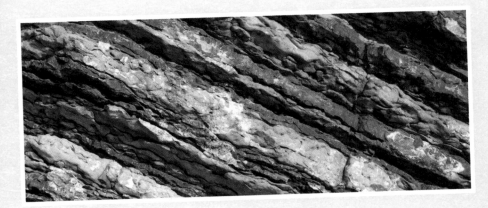

If you know the ages of sedimentary rock layers, and know where they are found, then you can hunt for fossils in them.

Even delicate insect wings can be found fossilized in sedimentary rocks.

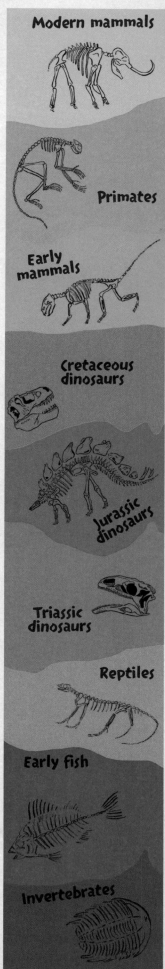

Modern mammals

Primates

Early mammals

CENOZOIC ERA

Cretaceous dinosaurs

Jurassic dinosaurs

Triassic dinosaurs

Reptiles

MESOZOIC ERA

Early fish

Invertebrates

PALEOZOIC ERA

WHAT DO PALEONTOLOGISTS DO?

Paleontologists are scientists who study the history of life on Earth by researching fossils. They often spend their time hunting for new fossils and bringing them back to museums to be preserved, or in laboratories preparing fossils for research.

STUDYING FOSSILS

By studying fossils, paleontologists can figure out what the animal looked like when it was alive, what species it was and even whether it is a new discovery!

Paleontologists predict where fossils might be found and organize dig teams to find them.

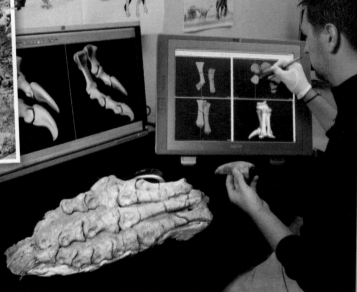

Paleontologists can also look at the features of fossils to find out how they're related to other fossils.

SOLVING THE PUZZLE

Paleontology also involves some biology. Paleontologists use what they know about modern animals to figure out what extinct animals would have been like when they were alive.

Looking at giraffes can help us imagine how similar dinosaurs, like this sauropod, moved.

We can even try to figure out how sauropods used their necks.

Modern paleontology is enhanced by computers. We now have the technology to create digital fossils using laser scanning.

The fossilized bones are scanned in 3D, using a laser.

A simulation can show how a dinosaur might have moved.

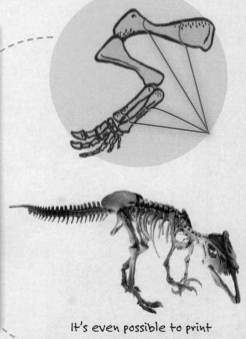

It's even possible to print a dinosaur in 3D!

11

REBUILDING SKELETONS

Fossils are quite unusual because not many dinosaurs died in exactly the right conditions to create them. Finding a complete dinosaur skeleton is very rare. Most of the time, paleontologists will find just a few bones, or a jumble of bones from different dinosaurs, all within the same area.

It takes whole teams of paleontologists to search areas to find as many fossils as possible.

FIND THE PIECES

Piecing the bones together to figure out what they came from can be tricky. Often we don't know what the animal looked like when it was alive. Paleontologists spend time figuring out what a whole dinosaur might have looked like, from just a few bones!

A GIANT JIGSAW PUZZLE

Luckily, we do sometimes find complete skeletons. These can be used as guides to help paleontologists figure out what other dinosaurs may have looked like and to help determine how different bones would have fit together.

Check out museums to see the amazing jigsaw of bones their teams have put together.

WHAT CAN WE LEARN?

Fossilized bones can teach us about dinosaurs. We can discover how they moved, how old they were when they died and how fast they grew.

Some bones even show signs of injuries, giving us clues about how the dinosaur died. By investigating bones in this way, we can learn what dinosaurs were like when they were alive.

By studying the features of a fossilized skull, paleontologists can figure out how a dinosaur lived and perhaps how it died.

13

THE TRIASSIC PERIOD

The Triassic (from about 252 to 201 million years ago) was the first period of the Mesozoic era. During this time, life on Earth was recovering from the largest mass extinction ever at the end of the Permian period (see page 6).

The extinction is thought to have been partly caused by the formation of the supercontinent Pangaea. All the existing continents crashed together to create one giant landmass.

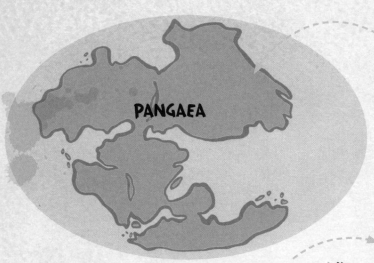

PANGAEA

This crash would have caused volcanic activity and disturbed many global systems, such as sea level and climate.

NEW SPECIES

The huge amount of volcanic activity at the end of the Permian period made life impossible for all but the toughest animals. It took some time after this extinction for life to recover, and this period saw the rise of many new animal groups, including:

Archosaurs
(pterosaurs; crocodiles;
dinosaurs and their
descendants, birds)

Early amphibians

Therapsids
(our mammal-like ancestors)

Turtles

THE FIRST DINOSAURS

There were three major dinosaur groups—sauropodomorphs, theropods and ornithischians—all of which first emerged in the Triassic period. These dinosaurs triumphed over other animals to become the dominant lifeform on land during the late Triassic and early Jurassic periods.

Theropods, like this Herrerasaurus, were meat-eaters and walked on their back legs.

Ornithischians, such as Pisanosaurus, had beaks and ate plants.

Sauropodomorphs, like Plateosaurus, had long necks and tails, and small heads.

LIFE IN THE SEA

Meanwhile, in the seas, prehistoric marine reptiles began to evolve, including unusual groups such as nothosaurs, plesiosaurs, ichthyosaurs and thalattosaurs.

Cymbospondylus, a type of ichthyosaur

Thallasiodracon, a plesiosaur

THE JURASSIC PERIOD

The Jurassic period lasted from approximately 201 to 145 million years ago. It was marked by the extinction of many reptile groups and the beginning of the time of the dinosaurs. Compared to the Triassic, the climate was more humid and tropical, similar to some parts of Africa and South America today.

Pangaea began to break apart and split into two large continents, Laurasia in the north, and Gondwana in the south.

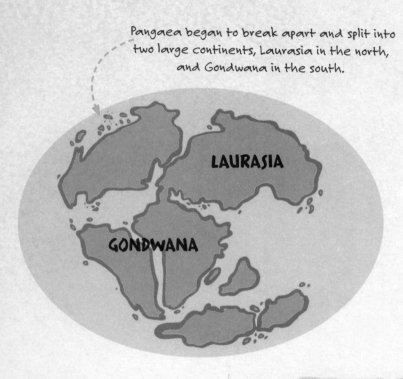

LAURASIA

GONDWANA

The climate was mainly tropical, encouraging new life to develop.

NEW SEA LIFE

The break-up of Pangaea created more coastal areas, which provided excellent conditions for new life to grow and develop into many forms.

In the oceans, reptiles such as ichthyosaurs, pliosaurs, plesiosaurs and crocodiles were supreme hunters.

OTHER NEW LIFE FORMS

Early lizards, frogs, salamanders and other amphibious groups began to develop during this period. Unusual crocodile-like animals called choristoderes existed, alongside a range of crocodiles including dwarf and marine species. Although early mammals did exist, they were not common at this time.

Frog

Salamander

Dwarf crocodile

Anchiornis,
a theropod

Mamenchisaurus,
a huge sauropod

NEW DINOSAUR GROUPS

This period saw a rise in the different types of dinosaurs. The result was a bizarre and wonderful array of animals, from the tiniest, nimblest runners like *Compsognathus* to towering sauropods like *Mamenchisaurus* and large predatory theropods such as *Allosaurus*.

Stegosaurus being attacked by a
predatory Allosaurus

17

THE CRETACEOUS PERIOD

The final period in the Mesozoic era, the Cretaceous period, lasted from approximately 145 to 66 million years ago. Pangaea had completely fragmented by this time into the continents we know now. The climate was warmer than it is today.

Inland seas covered much of North America and Europe was a large group of islands, with much of the land covered by shallow seas.

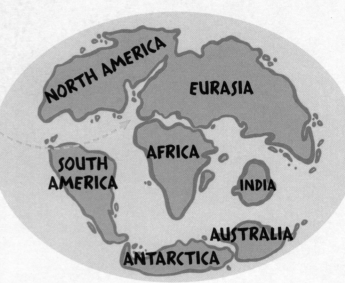

FIGHT FOR SURVIVAL

On land, birds and mammals began to multiply. The number of flying reptiles, pterosaurs, dropped as birds began to dominate the skies.

Avisaurus archibaldi was an early bird from the late Cretaceous period.

Beipiaosaurus was a bird-like theropod from the early Cretaceous period.

IN THE SEA

In the seas, the Jurassic marine reptiles were joined by mosasaurs, modern shark groups and rays.

This is a mosasaur, Tylosaurus proriger, attacking a shark from the species Cretoxyrhina mantelli.

THE LAST DINOSAURS

Dinosaurs such as *Tyrannosaurus rex* and *Triceratops* both lived during the late Cretaceous period. At the end of the Cretaceous period there was another mass extinction. This saw the end of all of the non—bird-like dinosaurs, as well as the marine reptiles and many other groups. Now it was the turn of mammals and birds to spread.

Fierce predator Tyrannosaurus rex and plant-eating Triceratops were among the last surviving dinosaurs.

FIELD GUIDE

The details on the 12 dinosaurs you will reconstruct are in
this section, starting with the most recent dinosaurs,
as if you were digging down through the ground.
Five dinosaurs are from the Cretaceous period, five are from
the Jurassic period and two are from the Triassic period.

You will find information on what they looked like, what
they ate, how they moved and where their fossils have been
found. To give you an idea of the height of each dinosaur,
look for either the tall shadow person (6 ft/1.8m)
or the small mouse (3 in/8cm).

ANKYLOSAURUS MAGNIVENTRIS

Ankylosaurus was a living, breathing tank with bony armor covering most of its body. Of all the ankylosaurs, *Ankylosaurus* was the biggest. It lived alongside mega-predators like *Tyrannosaurus rex*. Unlike its hadrosaurian (duck-billed) and ceratopsian (beaked and horned) cousins, *Ankylosaurus* did not have teeth for grinding food—it had leaf-shaped teeth for cropping plants.

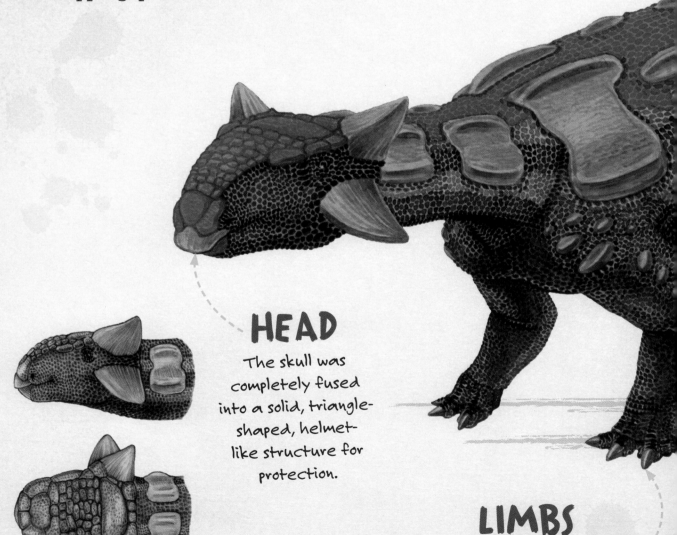

HEAD
The skull was completely fused into a solid, triangle-shaped, helmet-like structure for protection.

LIMBS
Short legs of equal length held the armored body close to the ground.

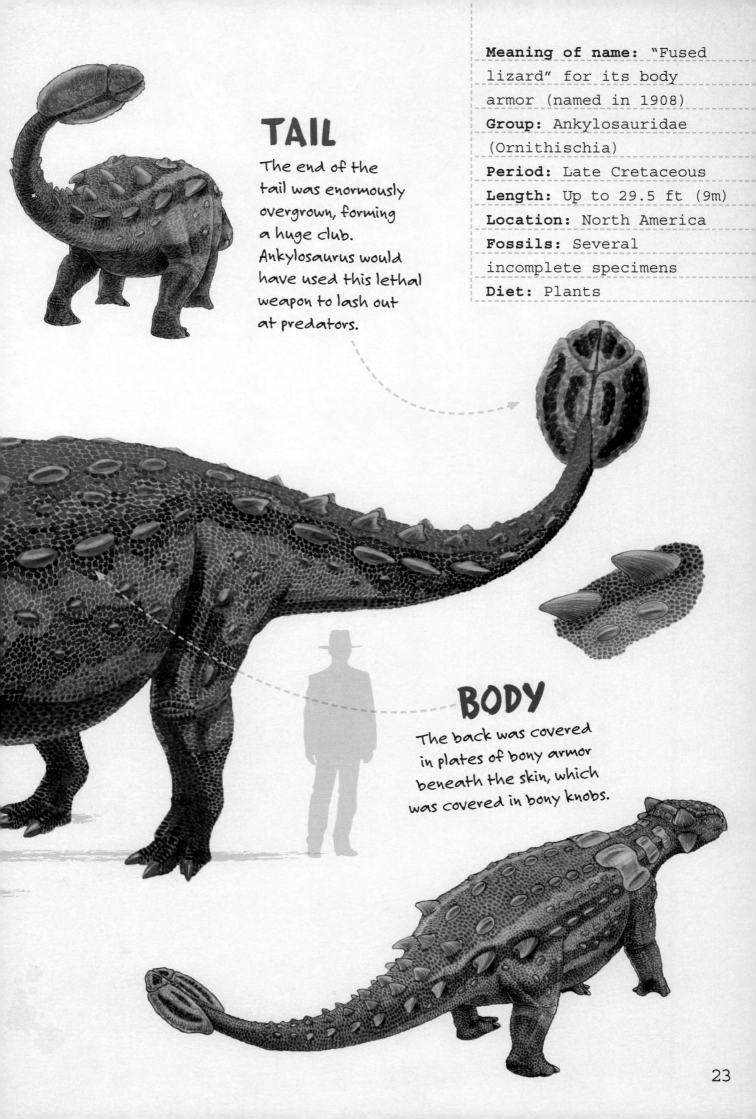

TAIL

The end of the tail was enormously overgrown, forming a huge club. Ankylosaurus would have used this lethal weapon to lash out at predators.

Meaning of name: "Fused lizard" for its body armor (named in 1908)
Group: Ankylosauridae (Ornithischia)
Period: Late Cretaceous
Length: Up to 29.5 ft (9m)
Location: North America
Fossils: Several incomplete specimens
Diet: Plants

BODY

The back was covered in plates of bony armor beneath the skin, which was covered in bony knobs.

PARASAUROLOPHUS WALKERI

Parasaurolophus is known for its long tube-shaped crest. The crest's shape may have changed as *Parasaurolophus* grew up, and might have differed between males and females. Early paleontologists thought the crest could have been a snorkel, and that *Parasaurolophus* might have been amphibious, but there is little evidence for this today.

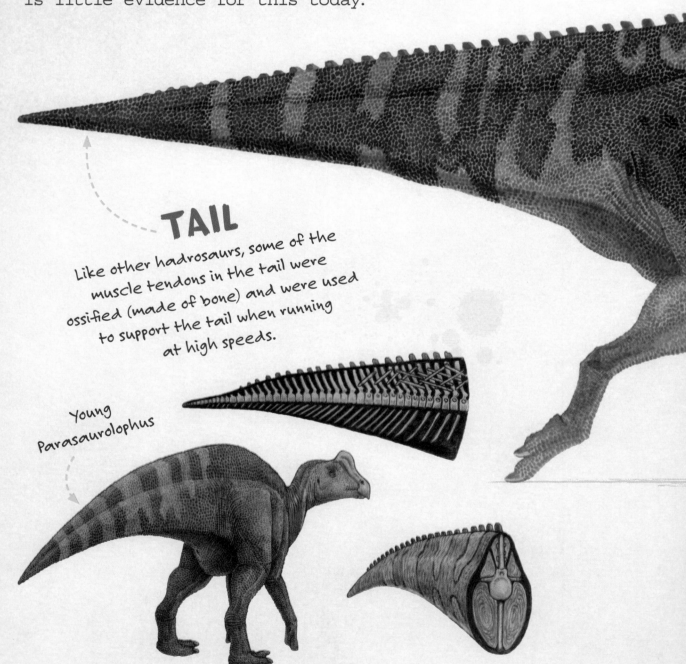

TAIL

Like other hadrosaurs, some of the muscle tendons in the tail were ossified (made of bone) and were used to support the tail when running at high speeds.

Young Parasaurolophus

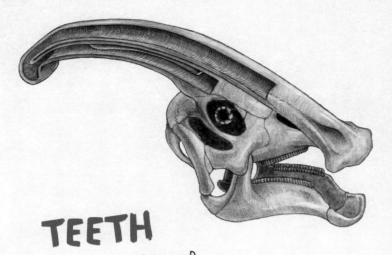

TEETH

The duck-shaped jaws of Parasaurolophus were filled with hundreds of teeth for grinding up the immense amounts of plants it needed to survive.

Meaning of name: "Near crested lizard" (named in 1922)

Group: Hadrosauridae (Ornithischia)

Period: Late Cretaceous

Length: Up to 33 ft (10m)

Location: Alberta, Canada

Fossils: One incomplete skeleton with a skull

Diet: Plants

BITESIZE FACT
Parasaurolophus probably used its long, hollow crest like a horn for communicating with other parasaurolophuses.

LIMBS

Parasaurolophus would usually walk on all four feet. If it wanted to move faster—to escape from a predator, for example—it could stand up and run on its hind limbs.

25

TRICERATOPS HORRIDUS

The hundreds of *Triceratops* found at the Hell Creek Formation fossil site in the USA make it one of the best-known dinosaurs. It is possible that it traveled in family groups rather than in herds, looking for plants to eat. The bony frill and horns were probably used for different activities, from display or communication to defense. Some of the fossils show that *Triceratops* battled with *Tyrannosaurus rex*.

LIMBS

With four stout limbs, Triceratops looked slow and heavy but could probably charge as ferociously as a rhinoceros!

BODY

The bulky body was built like a modern rhino or elephant.

26

Torosaurus is a bigger ceratopsian dinosaur from the same location. It could be a Triceratops, but at a more mature growth stage.

Torosaurus

Meaning of name:	"Three-horned face" (named in 1889)
Group:	Ceratopsidae (Ornithischia)
Period:	Late Cretaceous
Length:	Up to 29.5 ft (9m)
Location:	North America
Fossils:	Many complete and incomplete skeletons
Diet:	Plants

HORNS

Triceratops had a large, bony frill with two sharp horns above the eyes and a smaller horn above the nose, used in fighting for territory or a mate.

BEAK

Triceratops used its bony beak to pluck or strip food from plants before chewing them up with its teeth.

TYRANNOSAURUS REX

Tyrannosaurus rex is known as one of the largest and fiercest of the carnivorous dinosaurs. Paleontologists believe it hunted other dinosaurs for food, as well as scavenging from the carcasses left by other predators. At least 30 fossil specimens have been found.

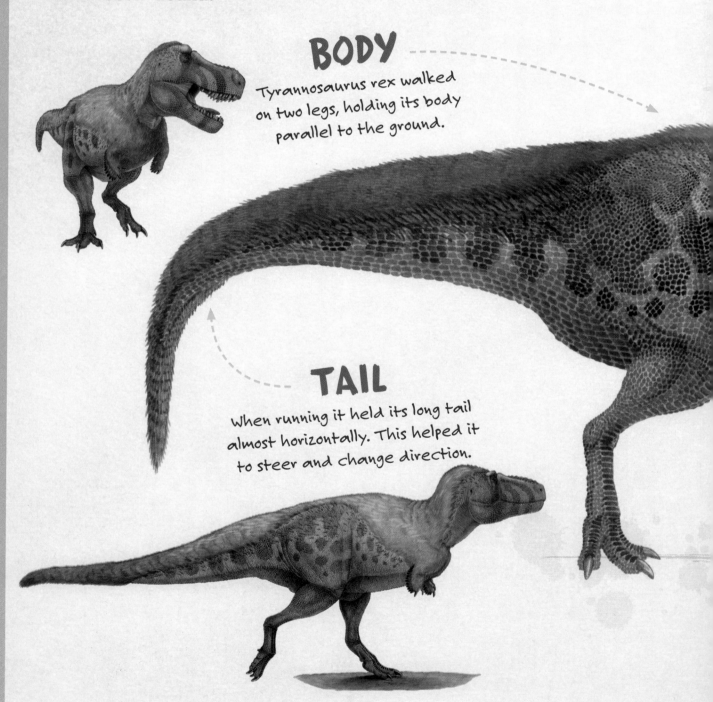

BODY

Tyrannosaurus rex walked on two legs, holding its body parallel to the ground.

TAIL

When running it held its long tail almost horizontally. This helped it to steer and change direction.

Scientists think T. rex may have been covered in "protofeathers." These simple hair-like structures were an early form of true feathers, like in most modern birds.

"Protofeathers" resembled the down of a baby chicken or the hairy feathers of an emu.

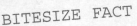

evolution of a feather

Meaning of name:	"Tyrant lizard king" (named in 1905)
Group:	Tyrannosauridae
Period:	Late Cretaceous
Length:	Up to 39 ft (13m)
Location:	North America
Fossils:	At least 30 specimens of varying completeness
Diet:	Meat

HEAD

The large, powerful skull was full of long stake-like teeth for puncturing flesh and bones.

LIMBS

The extremely short but strong arms ended in two clawed fingers. The long, clawed hind limbs allowed T. rex to run fast in short bursts.

BEIPIAOSAURUS INEXPECTUS

As its species name "*inexpectus*" suggests, *Beipiaosaurus* was an unexpected find. It had teeth like those of early sauropods, so it probably ate plants. This is unusual because most of its theropod cousins ate meat. It is one of many dinosaurs found in China that had feathers, but they were probably for warmth or display rather than for flying.

TAIL

The long tail was covered in thin, filament-like feathers, much like the rest of the body.

Yutyrannus

BITESIZE FACT
Until the discovery of Yutyrannus in 2012, Beipiaosaurus was the largest known feathered dinosaur.

BODY

The lightly built body had long, slender bones, similar to a modern-day ostrich.

Meaning of name: "Beipiao lizard," after the city in China (named in 1999)
Group: Therizinosauroidea (Theropoda)
Period: Early Cretaceous
Length: Up to 7 ft (2.2m)
Location: China
Fossils: At least two incomplete skeletons
Diet: Plants

BEAK

Like many ornithischian dinosaurs, Beipiaosaurus had a beak for plucking leaves from plants and trees.

LIMBS

The long, bird-like legs and short forelimbs ended in three claws.

ALLOSAURUS FRAGILIS

With its sharp teeth and the possibility that it hunted in groups, *Allosaurus* is known as the "wolf of the Jurassic." Known from the dinosaur fossil sites of the western USA, it probably preyed on dinosaurs such as *Stegosaurus* or, as an easier meal, the ornithopod *Camptosaurus*. One *Allosaurus* fossil even shows a healed wound where a *Stegosaurus* tail-spike had punctured it!

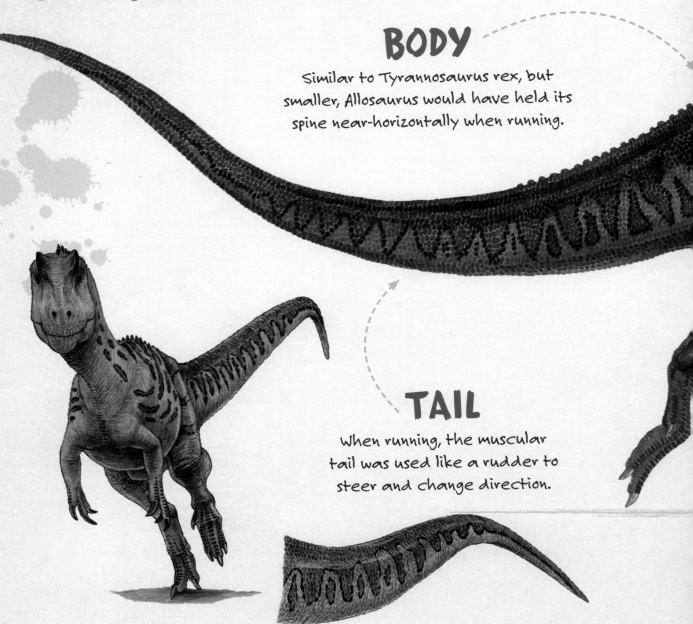

BODY

Similar to Tyrannosaurus rex, but smaller, Allosaurus would have held its spine near-horizontally when running.

TAIL

When running, the muscular tail was used like a rudder to steer and change direction.

EYE CRESTS

The little bony crests above the eyes were probably used to attract a mate or to identify other Allosauruses.

Meaning of name: "Different lizard" (named in 1877)

Group: Allosauridae (Theropoda)

Period: Late Jurassic

Length: Up to 39 ft (12m)

Location: North America

Fossils: Many complete and incomplete skeletons

Diet: Meat

TEETH

Allosaurus had dozens of razor-sharp teeth for slicing flesh. It probably used vertical, axe-like jaw movements when attacking prey.

LIMBS

An agile predator, Allosaurus ran on two powerful legs. It grasped prey with its three-clawed hands.

ANCHIORNIS HUXLEYI

Anchiornis fossils recently unearthed in China are so well-preserved that paleontologists have been able to reconstruct the color and pattern of their feathers. Along with other feathered dinosaurs such as *Microraptor*, *Anchiornis* probably couldn't fly but could glide. This shows that, at first, feathers probably evolved for reasons other than flight, such as gliding, warmth or signaling.

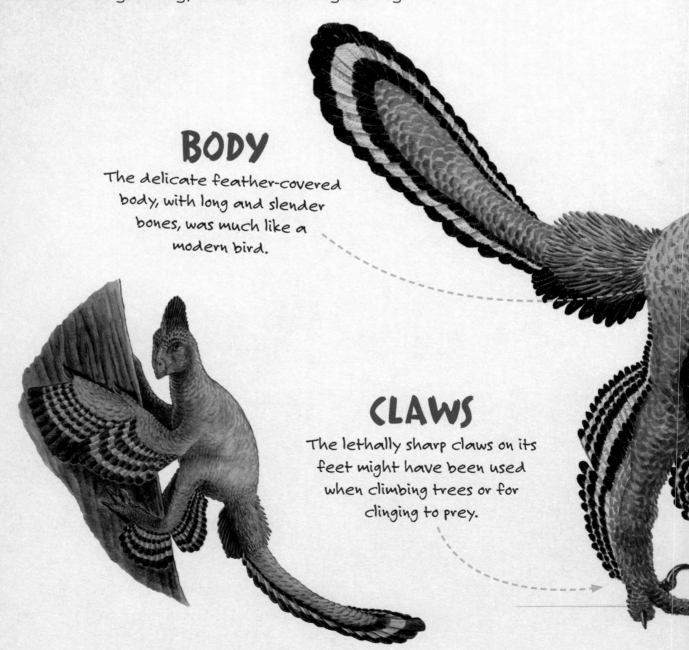

BODY

The delicate feather-covered body, with long and slender bones, was much like a modern bird.

CLAWS

The lethally sharp claws on its feet might have been used when climbing trees or for clinging to prey.

Along with *Aurornis xui*, *Anchiornis* may be one of the earliest ancestors of birds.

Meaning of name: "Near bird" (named in 2009)	
Group: Troodontidae (Theropoda)	
Period: Late Jurassic	
Length: Up to 20 in (50cm)	
Location: Liaoning, China	
Fossils: At least three (may be many in collections)	
Diet: Insects, small vertebrates	

CREST

The brownish orange head crest was probably used for signaling, or for attracting a mate.

WINGS

With its legs and arms forming wing-like structures, it is likely that *Anchiornis* glided down from the treetops to snatch up prey in its sharp claws.

STEGOSAURUS STENOPS

Many complete and incomplete skeletons of *Stegosaurus* have been found. It was alive during the Late Jurassic period, 150 to 155 million years ago. The name means "roof lizard," because when this dinosaur's bones were first discovered, some early reconstructions placed the rows of pointed bony plates flat on its back, like overlapping roof tiles.

HEAD

Stegosaurus had a tiny brain. It had a remarkably small skull for its body size, equipped with teeth for slicing vegetation. It held its head close to the ground.

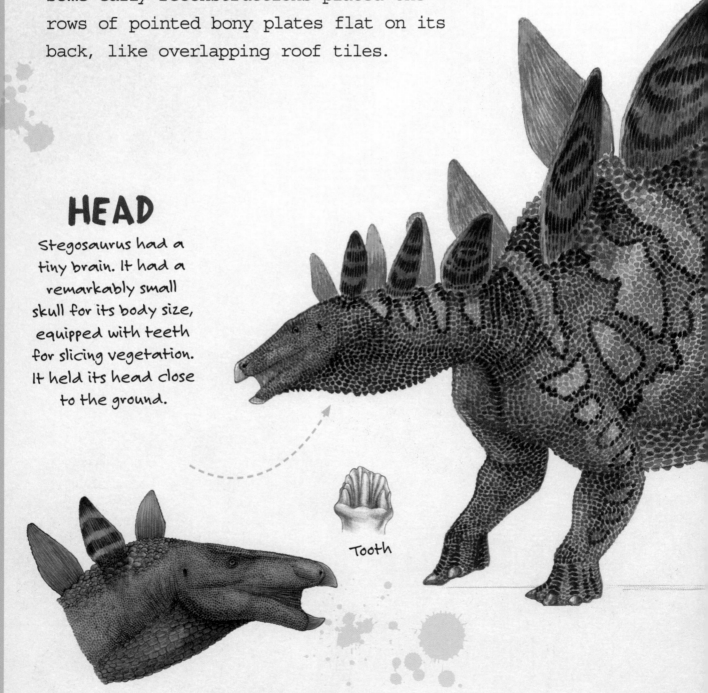

Tooth

Meaning of name: "Roof lizard" (named in 1877)
Group: Stegosauridae
Period: Late Jurassic
Length: Up to 30 ft (9m)
Location: North America
Fossils: Many complete and incomplete skeletons
Diet: Plants

TAIL

The tail was Stegosaurus's primary defensive weapon. The long, sharp, bony projections at the end were used in combat to spike enemies.

BODY

One of the most recognizable features are the plate-like bony shields along its back, possibly used for either display purposes or controlling body temperature.

LIMBS

Its hind limbs were slightly longer than its forelimbs, and it walked on all fours.

FRUITADENS HAAGARORUM

Named after Fruita, Colorado, the location in which it was found, *Fruitadens* was an odd little dinosaur. It measured between 26 and 29.5 inches (65 and 75 centimeters) long, and is the smallest of all known ornithischian dinosaurs. At approximately 150 million years old, it was one of the last surviving heterodontosaurs.

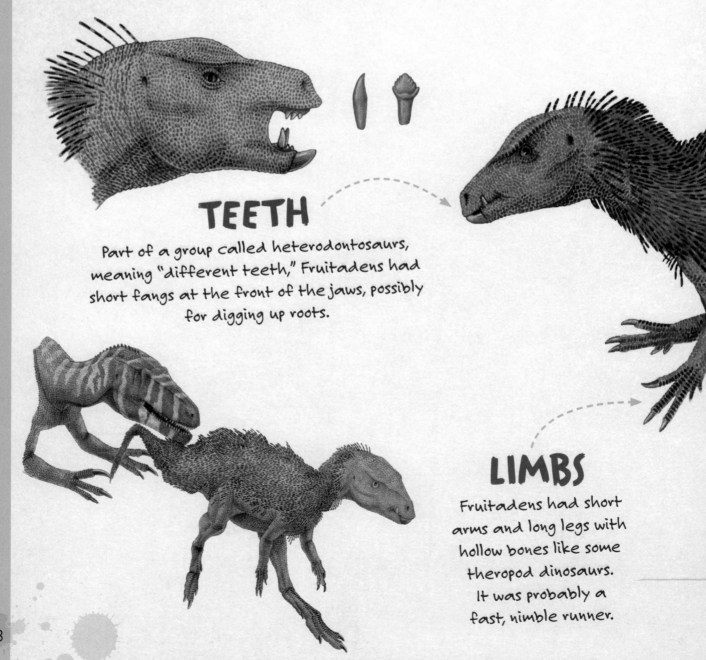

TEETH

Part of a group called heterodontosaurs, meaning "different teeth," Fruitadens had short fangs at the front of the jaws, possibly for digging up roots.

LIMBS

Fruitadens had short arms and long legs with hollow bones like some theropod dinosaurs. It was probably a fast, nimble runner.

BODY

The bristle-like features along parts of its body gave it an almost hedgehog-like appearance. It walked with a curved back.

Meaning of name: "Fruita tooth" (named in 2010)	
Group: Heterodontosauridae (Ornithischia)	
Period: Late Jurassic	
Length: 26.5–29.5 in (65–75cm)	
Location: Colorado, USA	
Fossils: Four skulls and partial skeletons	
Diet: Meat, plants, seeds	

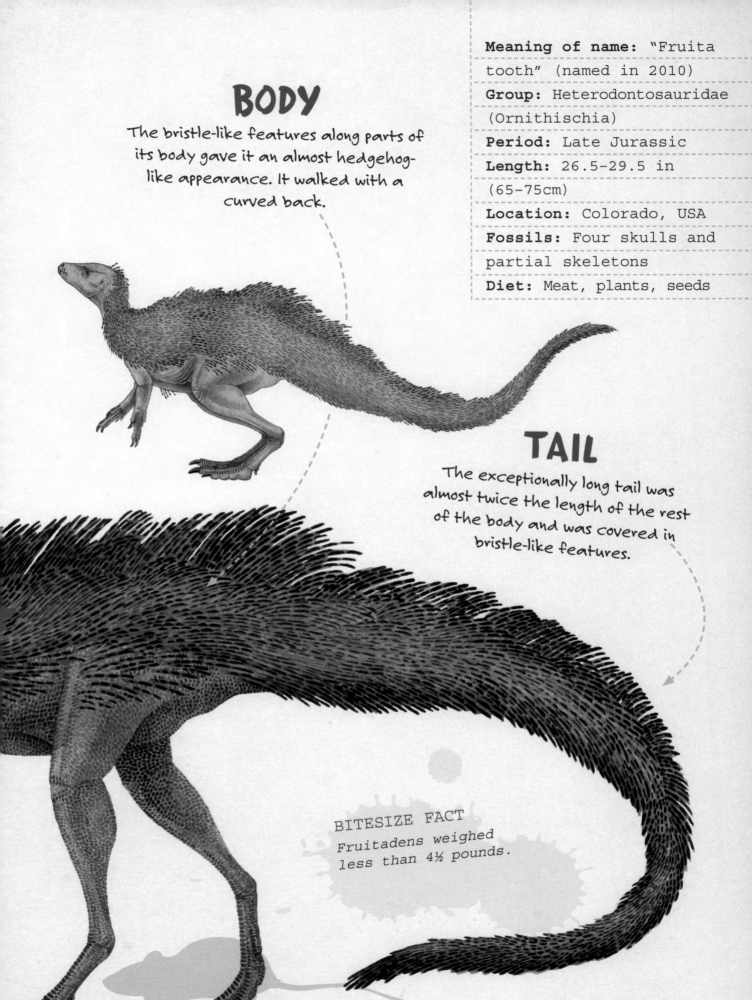

TAIL

The exceptionally long tail was almost twice the length of the rest of the body and was covered in bristle-like features.

BITESIZE FACT
Fruitadens weighed less than 4½ pounds.

GIRAFFATITAN BRANCAI

Sauropod dinosaurs were the largest animals to have walked the Earth and *Giraffatitan* was among the biggest. It had an enormous neck, which it held near-vertically, and its huge body was supported by four strong limbs. Two "nostrils" on top of its head near the tip of the snout meant that *Giraffatitan*, like *Parasaurolophus*, was originally thought to be amphibious. Current research, though, shows that water pressure would have crushed it, and it spent almost all of its time on land.

BODY

The enormous body was encased in long, sturdy ribs and positioned at an angle due to its longer forelimbs.

BITESIZE FACT

Many sauropods ate stones to help them grind up the tough plant food in their stomachs. These stones, called gastroliths, are often found with dinosaur skeletons.

TEETH

Its chisel-like teeth plucked large amounts of vegetation from plants, for processing in its enormous stomach.

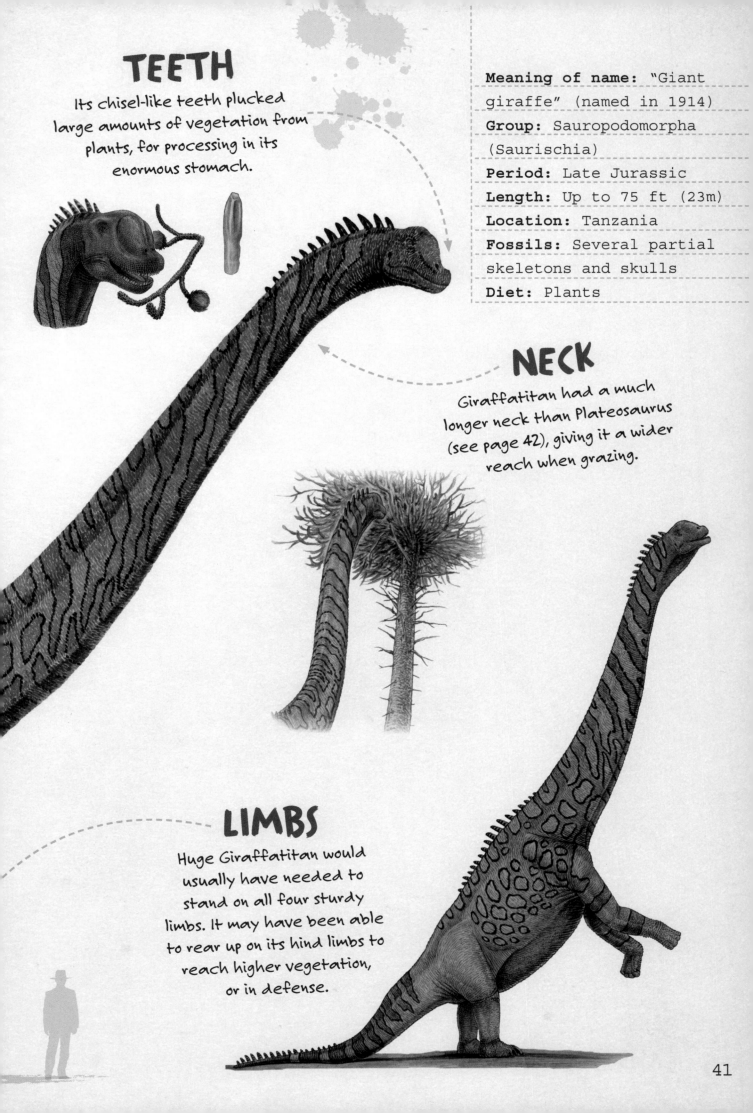

Meaning of name:	"Giant giraffe" (named in 1914)
Group:	Sauropodomorpha (Saurischia)
Period:	Late Jurassic
Length:	Up to 75 ft (23m)
Location:	Tanzania
Fossils:	Several partial skeletons and skulls
Diet:	Plants

NECK

Giraffatitan had a much longer neck than Plateosaurus (see page 42), giving it a wider reach when grazing.

LIMBS

Huge Giraffatitan would usually have needed to stand on all four sturdy limbs. It may have been able to rear up on its hind limbs to reach higher vegetation, or in defense.

PLATEOSAURUS ENGELHARDTI

Plateosaurus was one of the earliest sauropodomorph dinosaurs, cousins of advanced sauropod dinosaurs like *Giraffatitan*. It's often called a "prosauropod" (meaning "before the sauropods") because of this. *Plateosaurus* may have eaten small animals along with its usual plant diet. Its long neck and tail balanced it while it searched for food in trees, and it could run fast on its long hind limbs.

TAIL

Its long tail might have been used for swiping when fighting for a mate or territory, or for balance when reaching for food in trees.

NECK

A small skull and a long neck helped Plateosaurus to reach for food in trees.

Meaning of name:	"Broad lizard" (named in 1837)
Group:	Sauropodomorpha (Saurischia)
Period:	Late Triassic
Length:	Up to 33 ft (10m)
Location:	Central and northern Europe
Fossils:	More than 100 skeletons
Diet:	Plants

BODY

Far smaller than its cousin Giraffatitan, the body was more lightly built with slender, curving ribs.

LIMBS

Plateosaurus would have moved around on two feet. Its forelimbs were unusually strong, and it probably used its hands for grasping.

PISANOSAURUS MERTII

Pisanosaurus, like *Fruitadens*, is an early ornithischian dinosaur. It lived about 70 million years before *Fruitadens* in the Late Triassic period, in what is now Argentina. *Pisanosaurus* is a rare dinosaur. It inhabited the same area as the better-known theropod *Herrerasaurus*, which probably viewed *Pisanosaurus* as a tasty snack!

BITESIZE FACT
Pisanosaurus might be the earliest ancestor of all the ornithischian dinosaurs.

TAIL
Using its long tail for balance, Pisanosaurus, like Fruitadens, could run fast to avoid predators.

BITESIZE FACT
Unlike earlier dinosaurs, two of Pisanosaurus's three hip bones pointed backward and downward.

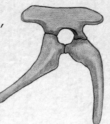

BODY

Pisanosaurus was probably the first dinosaur to have a "bird-hipped" arrangement of hip bones instead of a "lizard-hipped" arrangement. It had a sleek body almost like a modern greyhound.

Meaning of name:	"Pisano lizard," for the paleontologist Juan Pisano (named in 1967)
Group:	Ornithischia
Period:	Late Triassic
Length:	Up to 3.3 ft (1m)
Location:	Argentina
Fossils:	One incomplete skeleton
Diet:	Plants

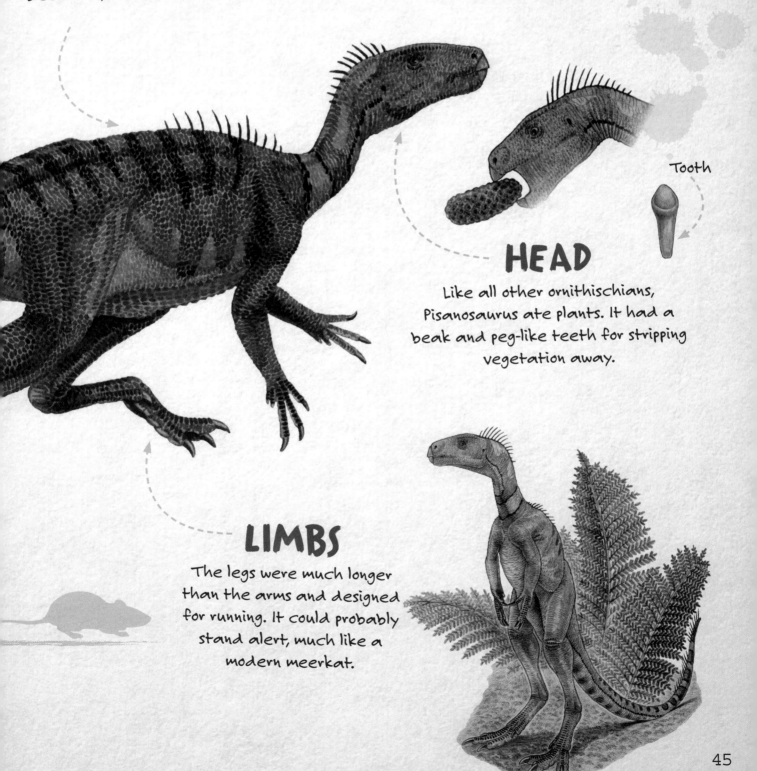

Tooth

HEAD

Like all other ornithischians, Pisanosaurus ate plants. It had a beak and peg-like teeth for stripping vegetation away.

LIMBS

The legs were much longer than the arms and designed for running. It could probably stand alert, much like a modern meerkat.

DINOSAUR DIGS

Bones belonging to the 12 dinosaurs in the Field Guide have been uncovered at three different dig sites but they are all mixed up! Your job is to figure out how to reconstruct each dinosaur's skeleton.

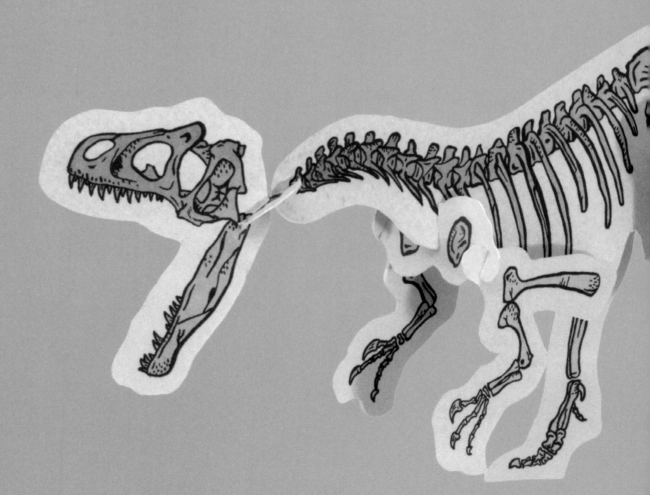

The dig sites are from three different time periods—
the Cretaceous, the Jurassic and the Triassic. Use the
descriptions in the Field Guide section to help you
identify which bones belong to which dinosaur.

Before you begin, look at the next two pages
for information on constructing your
pop-out models.

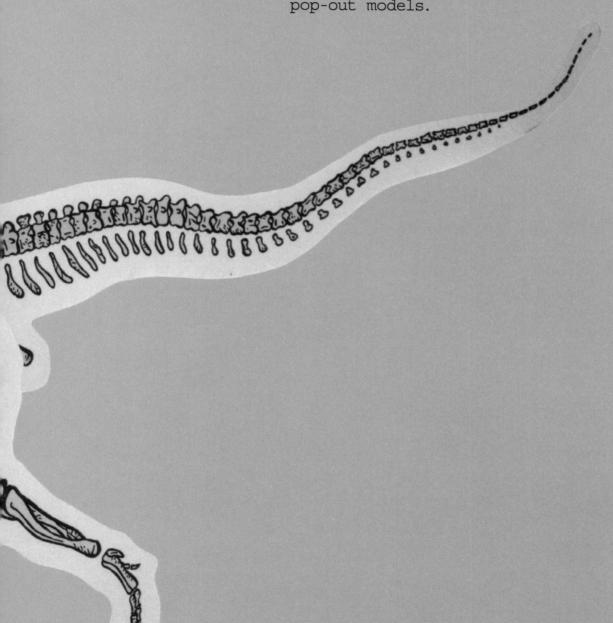

CONSTRUCTING YOUR MODEL DINOSAURS

To build your models, you need to determine which bones belong to which dinosaur. It's a good idea to pop out the named model stands first and then, as you collect a set of bones, match them with their stand. Do one era at a time so you don't get confused!

Identify the pieces

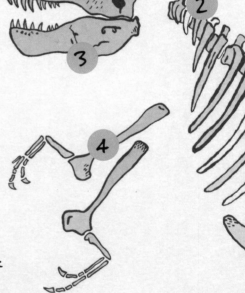

1 Pop out the stands and fold back the flap at the dotted line.

2 Pop out the bodies. Look out for things such as bony plates, a long, thick tail or a slim, bird-shaped skeleton.

3 Identify the heads. Look for features like horns, a bony crest or unusual teeth.

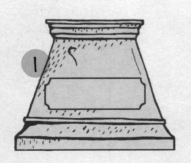

4 Look for arms that are the same size. Check for matching claws and the correct number of toes.

5 Identify legs that are the same size. Check to be sure that the length, thickness and the feet all match.

Putting it all together

- The pieces fit together with slots—slide the slots together gently.

- Attach the heads and tails first. Join the smallest bone on the neck piece to the head, and the biggest to the body.

- Attach the hip bones and shoulder bones (if needed) and then the limbs.

- Place the dinosaur in the stand where marked on the body or tail (one is on the head!) and you have your very own model dinosaur!

- To help your dinosaurs stand still, you can glue or tape the stands to some thick cardboard.

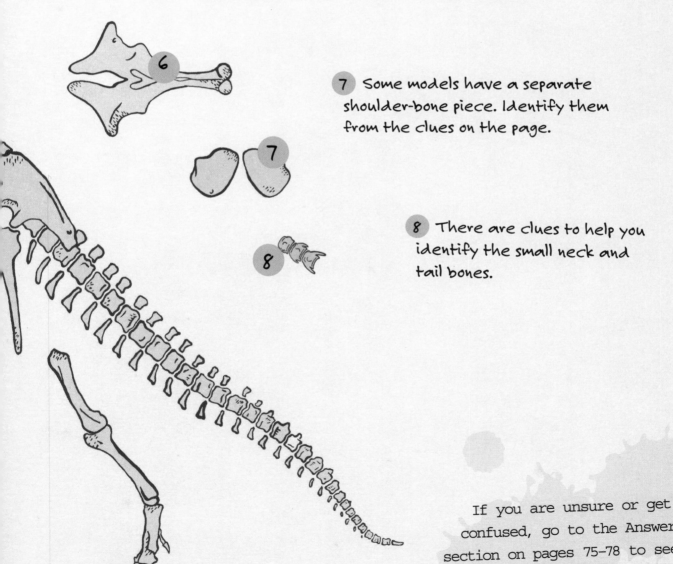

6 Some models have a separate hip-bone piece. Identify them from the clues on the page.

7 Some models have a separate shoulder-bone piece. Identify them from the clues on the page.

8 There are clues to help you identify the small neck and tail bones.

If you are unsure or get confused, go to the Answers section on pages 75–78 to see if you are on the right track.

Hints!

- Start with the Triassic dinosaurs—there are only two of them!

- Read the Field Guide pages for each dinosaur and study the pictures.

- Think about the shape and size of each dinosaur. A large animal will have larger, thicker bones. A light, long-legged dinosaur will have bones to match.

- Don't forget the small details. Watch for things like claws, feet or a beak.

- Sections that face front-to-back are not identical on both sides. Sections that face side-to-side are identical.

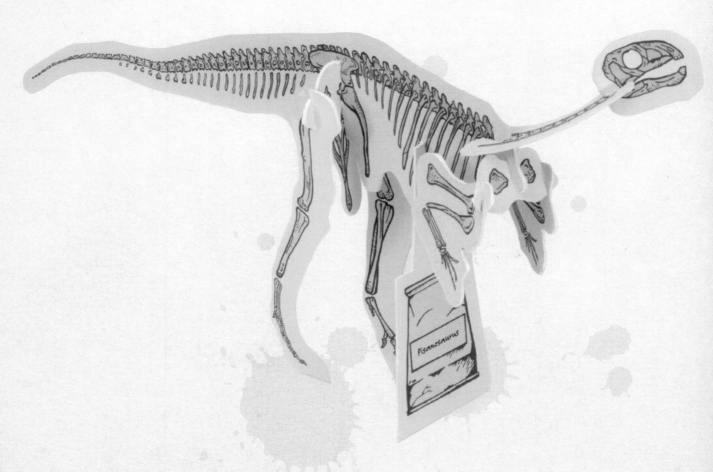

Answers

Stegosaurus

Page 65

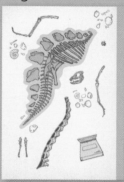

Page 67

Page 69

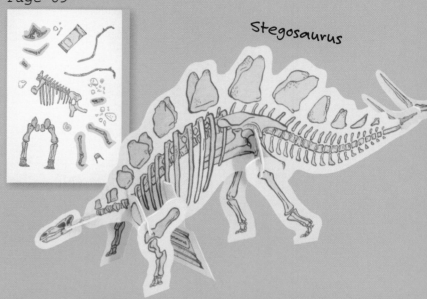

Stegosaurus

DIG SITE 3: TRIASSIC PERIOD

Pisanosaurus

Page 71

Page 73

Pisanosaurus

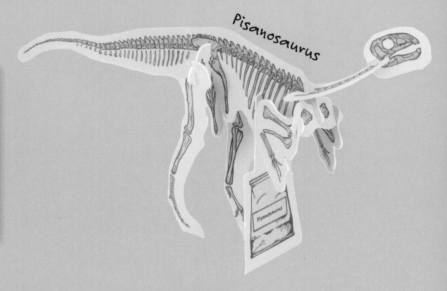

Plateosaurus

Page 71

Page 73

Plateosaurus

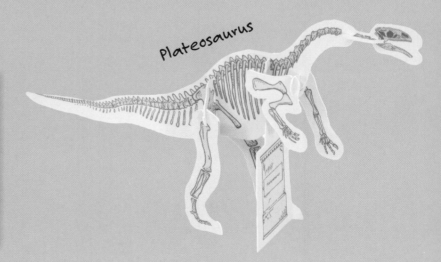

Answers

Anchiornis

Anchiornis

Page 63

Page 67

Page 69

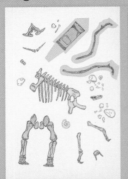

Fruitadens

Fruitadens

Page 61

Page 63

Page 65

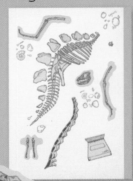

Page 67

Giraffatitan

Giraffatitan

Page 61

Page 63

Page 65

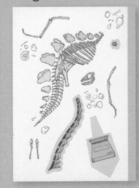

Page 67

Page 69

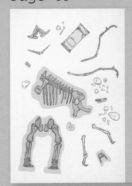

Acknowledgments

Jonathan Tennant would like to thank Jan Freedman, Joseph Hancock, Megan Shersby and Sally-Ann Spence for helpful comments as this book progressed. And everyone else for cheerleading :)

Vladimir Nikolov would like to thank Scott Hartman and Ville Sinkkonen. Their illustrative reconstructions of dinosaur skeletons were used as the scientific basis for many of the artworks in this book.

Photo credits

p8 – top: Shutterstock/ChinalletoPhoto; bottom: Shutterstock/Clive Watkins; bottom left: Shutterstock/alice-photo.
p9 – top: Shutterstock/dexns; middle: Shutterstock/Darren Foard; bottom: Shutterstock/Marcel Clemens.
p10 – top: Wikimedia Commons; middle: Shutterstock/ChameleonsEye; bottom: Science Photo Library/Pascal Goetgheluck.
p11 – top: Shutterstock/Vadim Petrakov; bottom left: Shutterstock/David Herraez Calzada; bottom right: Shutterstock/Lefteris Papaulakis.
p12 – top left: Shutterstock/chromographs; top right: Shutterstock/hans engbers; bottom: Science Photo Library/Joseph Nettis.
p13 – top: Shutterstock/Jorg Hackemann; middle: Wikimedia Commons.

Glossary

Amphibian An animal able to live both on land and in water at some time in its life cycle.

Ancestor An earlier creature from which a modern animal developed.

Ankylosaurs Herbivorous dinosaurs with bony armor covering both body and skull.

Archosaurs Birds, crocodiles and their ancestors, which include dinosaurs.

Ceratopsians Plant-eating dinosaurs with bony head-shields and triangular beaks.

Descendant The animal that has developed from a specific **ancestor.**

Extinction The dying out of an animal species.

Fossils The remains or traces of ancient animals and/or plants.

Gondwana The southern supercontinent that existed during the time of the dinosaurs.

Heterodontosaurs Early **ornithischian** dinosaurs.

Ichthyosaurs Swimming reptiles, which looked similar to dolphins.

Laurasia The northern supercontinent that existed during the time of the dinosaurs.

Mesozoic The age of the dinosaurs, roughly 252 to 66 million years ago.

Nothosaurs Unusual swimming reptiles from the Triassic period.

Ornithischians The "bird-hipped" dinosaurs, one major dinosaur group.

Ornithopods One of the most successful and varied groups of **ornithischians**.

Paleontologists People who study the history of life on Earth.

Pangaea The Earth's supercontinent when all land was joined together, from approximately 270 to 200 million years ago.

Plesiosaurs Marine reptiles, often with long necks and paddle-like fins.

Pterosaurs Flying reptiles with wings made of a thin layer of skin and long bones.

Saurischians The "lizard-hipped" dinosaurs, including the ancestors of all birds.

Sauropods The enormous plant-eating dinosaurs with long tails and necks.

Sedimentary rock A layered type of rock, such as sandstone, in which fossils are usually found.

Thalattosaurs Unusual Triassic reptiles, with long, powerful tails for swimming.

Therapsids Members of a family of animals that includes mammals and their **ancestors**.

Theropods A group of mostly meat-eating dinosaurs—also all modern-day birds.

Paleontologist's Notes

Paleontologist's Notes